Bible Story Nixon, Joan Lowery

WHO IS MY NEIGHBOR?

Property of The
FAITH REFORMED CHURCH
ZEELAND, MICHIGAN

FAITH REFORMED CHURCH
LIBRARY RULES

Please keep this book clean and do not lose pages.

Do not lend book to others.

A fee of 5 cents a week will be charged on each book not returned within 2 weeks.

No book will be issued to any person incurring such a fee until it has been paid.

WHO IS MY NEIGHBOR?

The Good Samaritan for Beginning Readers

Luke 10:29-37 FOR CHILDREN

by Joan Lowery Nixon
illustrated by Aline Cunningham

I CAN READ A BIBLE STORY
Series Editor: Dorothy Van Woerkom

Publishing House
St. Louis

WITH LOVE TO MY
NIECE, CATHLIN COLLINS

Concordia Publishing House, St. Louis, Missouri
Copyright © 1976 Concordia Publishing House

Manufactured in the United States of America

Library of Congress Cataloging in Publication Data

Nixon, Joan Lowery.
    Who is my neighbor?

    (I can read a Bible story)
    1. Good Samaritan (Parable)—Juvenile literature. I. Cunningham, Aline. II. Title.
BT378.G6N59   226'.4'09505   76-13232
ISBN 0-570-07310-3
ISBN 0-570-07304-9 pbk.

Everywhere He went,

Jesus taught the people.

Many came to listen.

Many had questions to ask.

One day,

the people sat on the ground

to listen to Jesus.

A lawyer stood up.

He asked Jesus a question.

"Teacher," he said,
"how can I
get to heaven?"

Jesus said, "You are a lawyer. What does the law say?"

The man said,

"You shall love the Lord your God.

And you shall love your

neighbor."

Jesus said, "Your answer is right.

Love God.

Love your neighbor.

Then you shall live

forever in heaven."

But the man asked another question.

"Who is my neighbor?" he said.

So Jesus told the people

a story to show

what a neighbor is.

He told this story of

the Good Samaritan.

A man was walking alone on a winding, dusty road between two cities.

He walked down a steep hill
and around large, high rocks.
The sun was warm on his back.
Little curls of dust
flew from under his feet
as he walked.

All at once a band of robbers
jumped out
from behind the rocks.
"Give us your money!"
they shouted.

The man was frightened.

He gave them his money.

But this was not enough for them.

They tore off his cloak and his robe
to sell in the market place.

The robbers beat the man.
They threw him down
by the side of the road.
They left him there
and hurried away.

In a little while

a priest came down the road.

He had many things to do,

and he was in a hurry.

He pulled his cloak around his head
to keep out the sun
and the dust of the road.
He wished his donkey
could go faster!

He saw the man

lying

by the side of the road.

He stopped his donkey

and looked down at the man.

Then he shook his head.

He did not have time to stop.

The priest hurried on.

Soon someone else
came down the road.
He was a man who
took care of the temple.
His job was important.
He saw the hurt man,
but he had no time to stop.
He hurried on his way.

Then a man came

from the country of Samaria.

He was called a Samaritan.

He rode on a strong brown donkey.

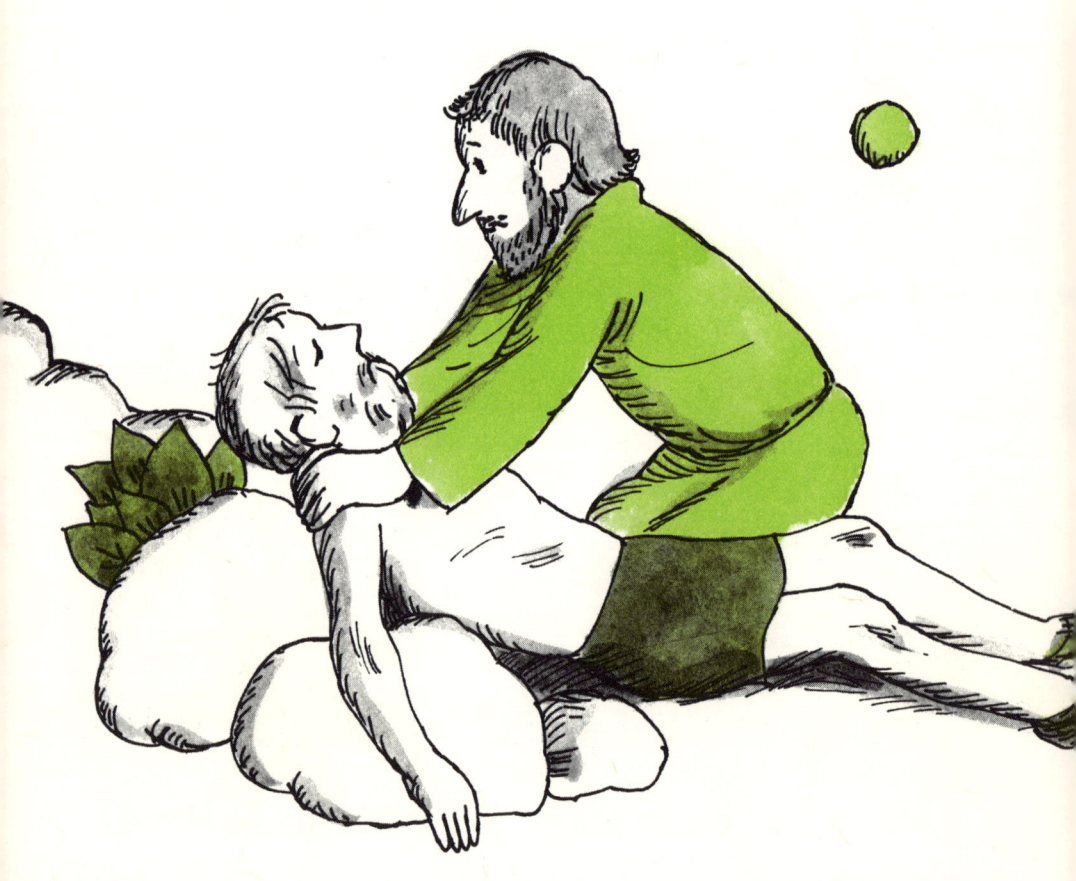

He saw the man

lying at the side of the road.

The Samaritan

felt sorry for this man.

He stopped to help him.

The Samaritan opened
his saddle bags.
He took out pieces of cloth,
and oil and wine.
He cleaned the man's wounds
with the oil.
He gave the man wine to drink.

The man was heavy.

The Samaritan had to work hard to lift him.

He carried the man
to his donkey
and laid him carefully
on the donkey's back.

The Samaritan walked slowly, leading the donkey.

They followed the winding road
down the side of the hill.
The rocks along the way
made long shadows
in the afternoon sun.

At last they came to an inn.

The Samaritan asked for a room.

He put the man into bed

and tried to make him feel better.

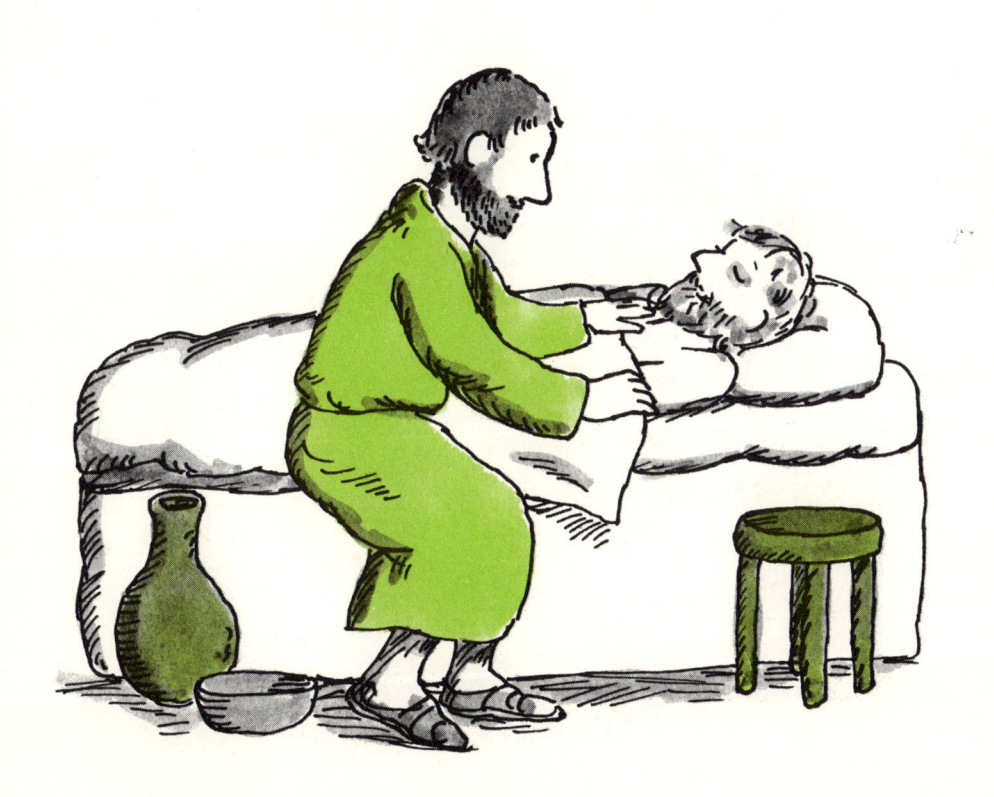

He stayed with the man

all night long,

taking care of him.

Morning came.

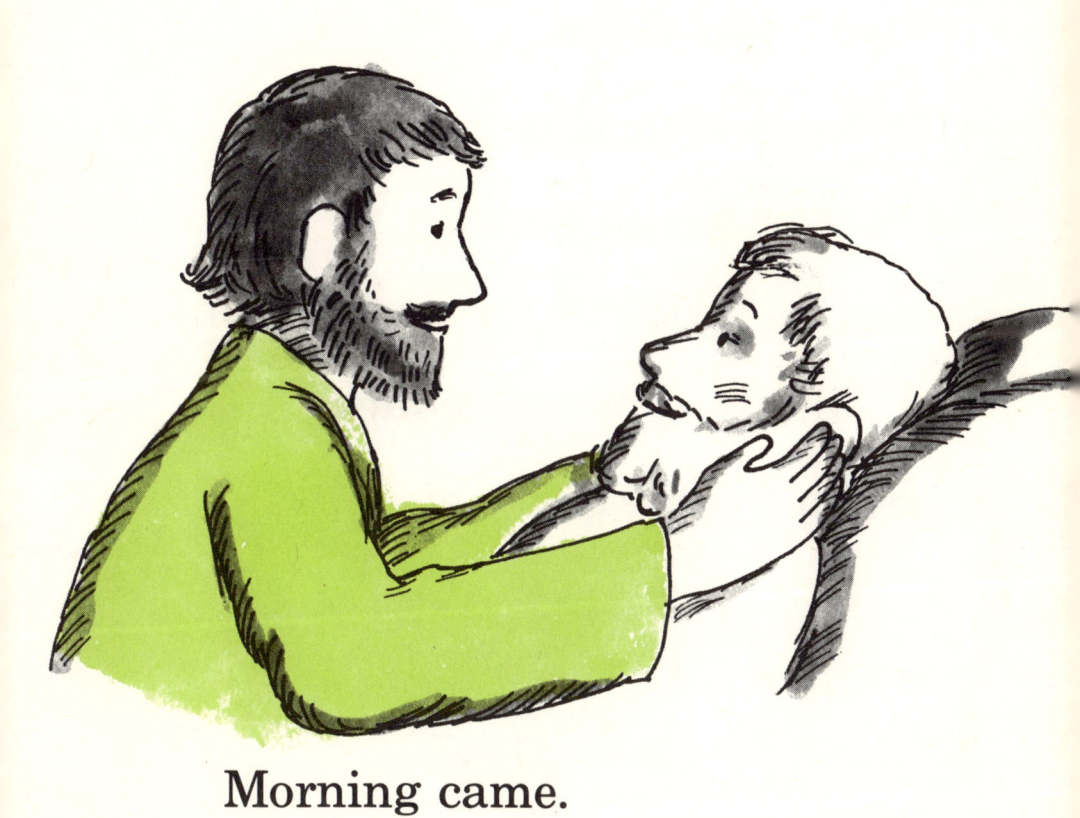

The Samaritan saw that the man was much better.

He was not going to die.

So he gave the innkeeper
two silver coins.
"Please look after this man,"
he said to the innkeeper.
"And if you need more than this,
I will give you the money
when I come back this way."

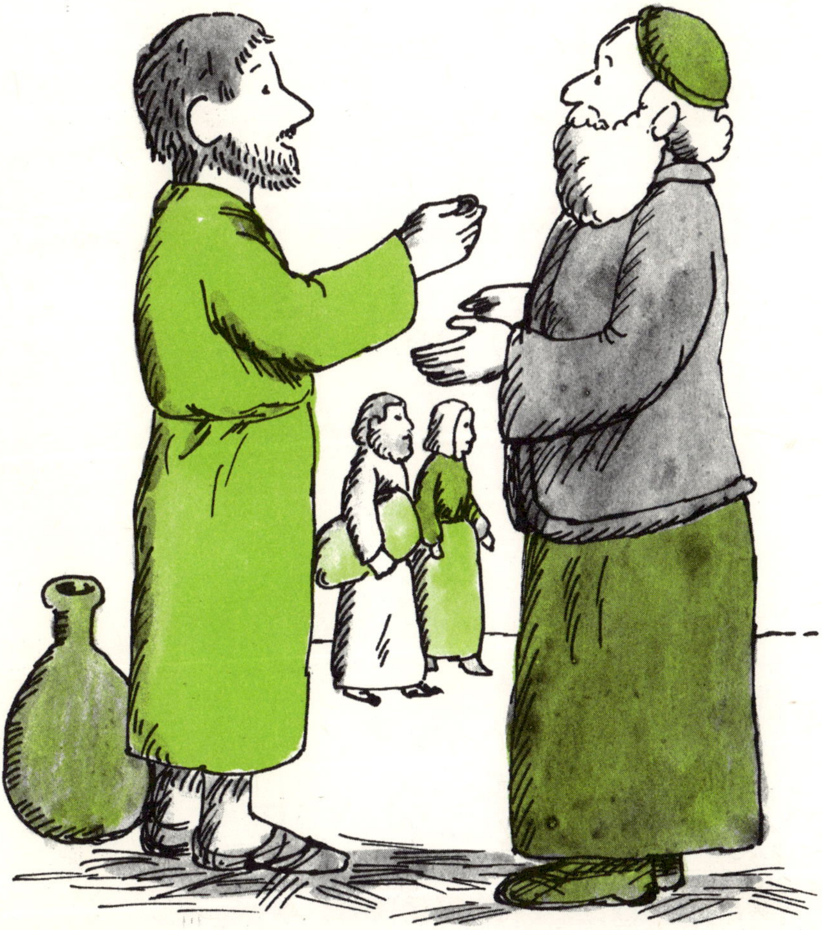

That was how
Jesus ended His story.
Then he said to the lawyer,
"Three men
saw the man who was hurt
by the robbers.
Which one do you think
was the man's neighbor?"

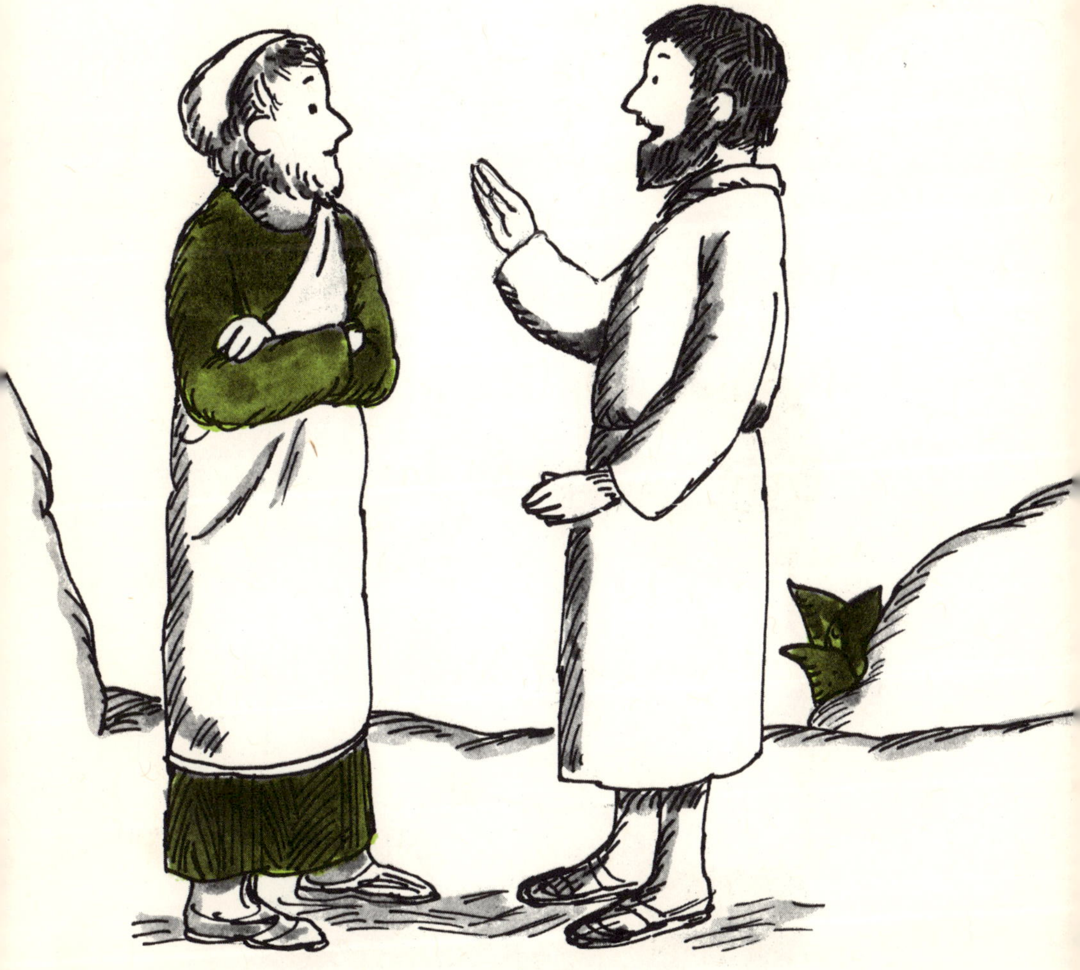

The lawyer answered quickly, "The one who took care of him— the Samaritan."

Jesus said to him,

"Then go and do what the

Samaritan did.

Go and help others,

as you would want them to help you."

The people got up from the ground.

They brushed the dust

from their robes.

Each one went home,
thinking about
what Jesus had said.
Each one went home
thinking,
"Who is MY neighbor?"

ABOUT THE AUTHOR

Joan Lowery Nixon has been a free-lance writer in magazine fiction and nonfiction for twenty-five years. She is the author of ten books for children, including *The Alligator Under the Bed,* which won the 1975 Texas Institute of Letters Award, and *The Mysterious Red Tape Gang,* which received a Certificate of Honor from the Mystery Writers of America at their Edgar Awards presentation in 1975. *The Secret Box Mystery,* her first book for beginning readers, was a Junior Literary Guild Selection. Ms. Nixion has also written several beginning science books in collaboration with her husband Hershell. The Nixons have four children and live in Houston.